WELCOME TO
JASORASSIC PARK

Other FoxTrot Books by Bill Amend

FoxTrot
Pass the Loot
Black Bart Says Draw
Eight Yards, Down and Out
Bury My Heart at Fun-Fun Mountain
Say Hello to Cactus Flats
May the Force Be With Us, Please
Take Us to Your Mall
The Return of the Lone Iguana
At Least This Place Sells T-Shirts
Come Closer, Roger, There's a Mosquito on Your Nose

Anthologies

FoxTrot: The Works
FoxTrot en masse
Enormously FoxTrot
Wildly FoxTrot
FoxTrot Beyond a Doubt

Welcome to Jasorassic Park

A FoxTrot Collection by Bill Amend

Andrews McMeel
Publishing

Kansas City

FoxTrot is distributed internationally by Universal Press Syndicate.

Information about Andrews McMeel Publishing can be found at www.andrewsmcmeel.com

98 99 00 01 02 BAH 10 9 8 7 6 5 4 3 2 1

ISBN: 0-8362-5183-0

Library of Congress Catalog Card Number: 97-80773

Visit *FoxTrot* on the World Wide Web at www.foxtrot.com

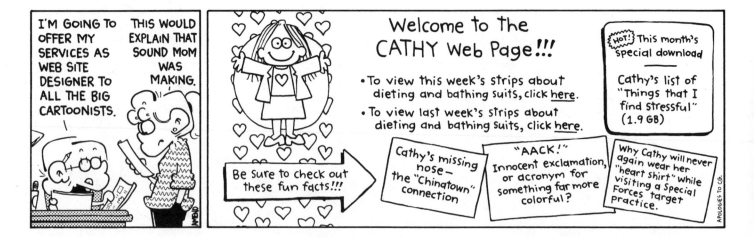

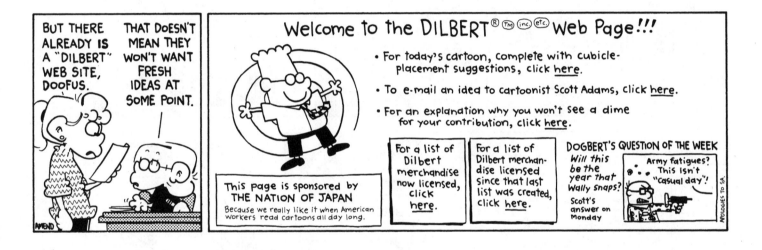

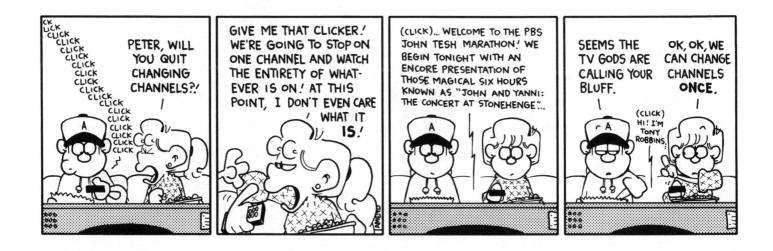

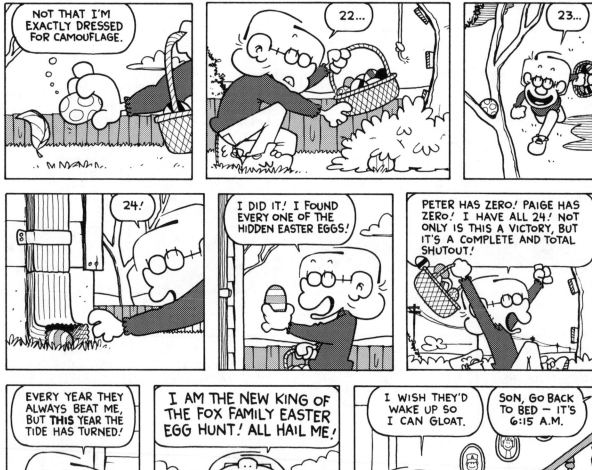

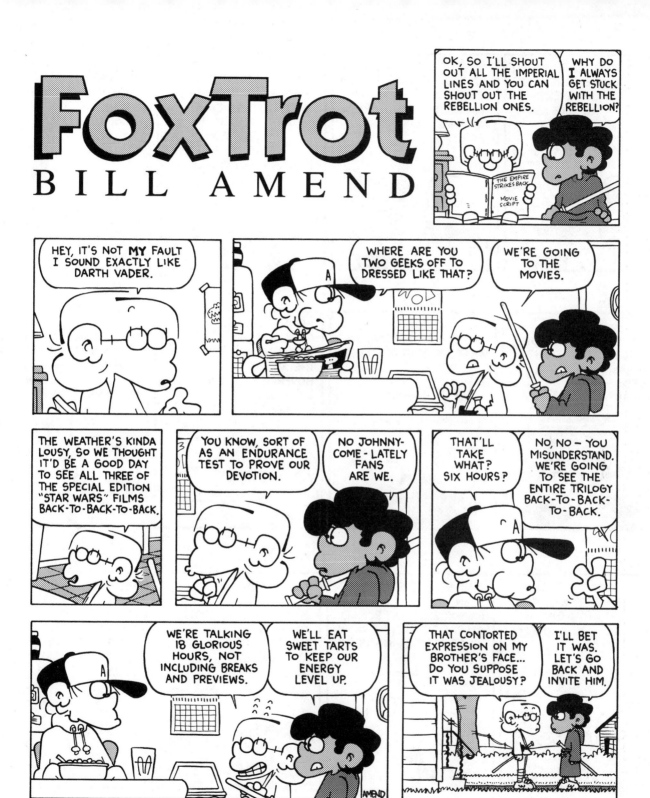

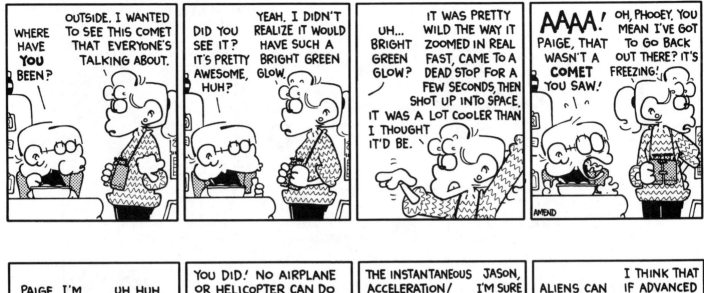

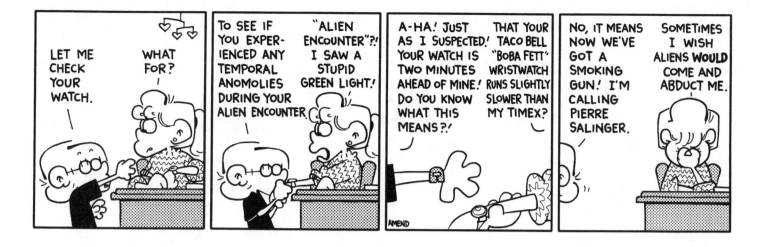

FoxTrot
BILL AMEND

FoxTrot

BILL AMEND

35

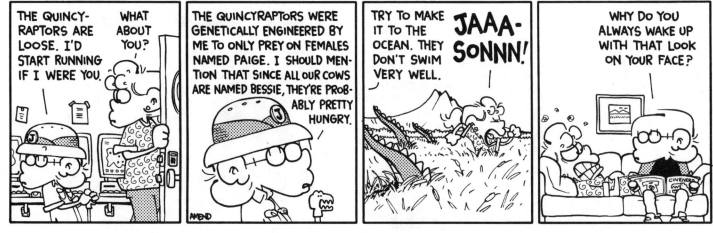

41

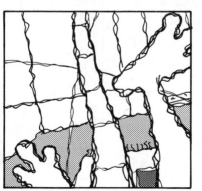

PAIGE! PAIGE! I GOT A JOB FOR THE SUMMER!

GET OUT! WHERE?!

AT THE PAVILIONPLEX-22 MOVIE THEATER! I FILLED OUT AN APPLICATION LAST WEEK AND THEY JUST CALLED TO SAY I CAN START TOMORROW!

COOL.

JUST THINK! ME... IN THE **FILM INDUSTRY!** I ALWAYS KNEW THAT IF I HELD OUT LONG ENOUGH, A DREAM JOB LIKE THIS WOULD SOMEDAY COME MY WAY!

ORDINARILY, I'D START YOU ON THE RESTROOM STALLS, BUT WE'VE GOT MAJOR SODA SPILLAGE IN THEATER 18.

WHY DID YOU ASK IF I OWNED KNEE PADS?

FOX, THEATERS 1 THROUGH 7 NEED CLEANING.

PETER, THEATERS 8 THROUGH 15 NEED CLEANING.

FOX, THEATERS 16 THROUGH 22 NEED CLEANING.

FINALLY, THEY'LL ALL BE DONE.

THEATERS 1 THROUGH 7 ARE READY FOR CLEANING AGAIN.

I'M BEGINNING TO SEE A REAL DOWNSIDE TO THIS JOB.

HOW'S PETER'S MOVIE THEATER JOB GOING?

JUST GREAT, FROM WHAT HE TELLS ME.

HE SAYS THEY MAY EVEN LET HIM WORK THE CONCESSION STAND TONIGHT.

HE SHOULD DO WELL AT THAT. WE FOXES ARE NATURAL SALESMEN.

REALLY? HE STRIKES ME AS BEING JUST A LITTLE TOO HONEST.

WOULD YOU LIKE OUR CHEESE-LIKE SAUCE ON YOUR NACHOS, OR SOME OILY FAKE BUTTER ON YOUR POPCORN, MA'AM?

PETER, MAY I SPEAK TO YOU FOR A SECOND?

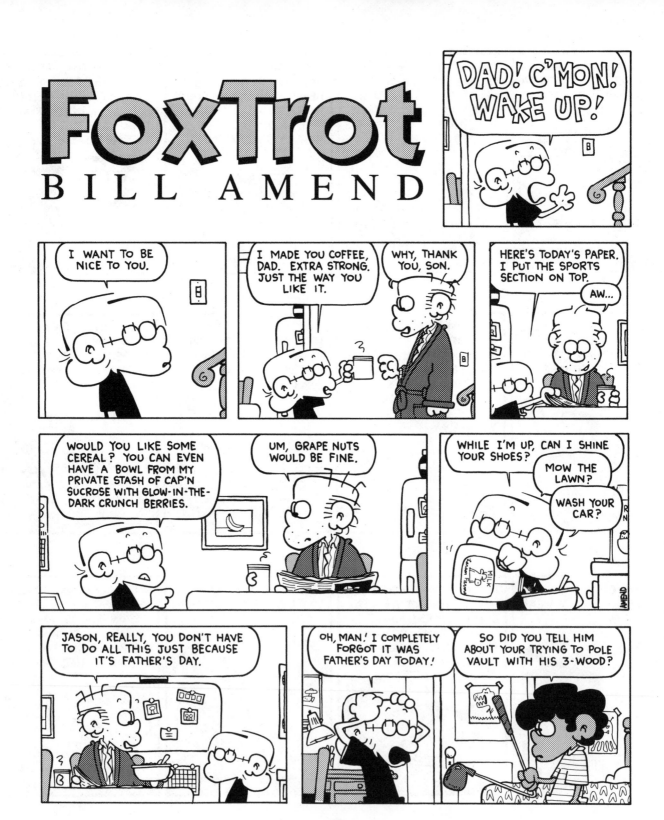

YOU KNOW, SWEETIE, MAYBE THIS SCIENCE CAMP WOULD BE GOOD FOR JASON.

HE'D BE WITH OTHER BRIGHT KIDS... SURROUNDED BY NATURE GETTING FRESH AIR... STUDYING SOMETHING HE LOVES...

BUT HE'S JUST SO YOUNG.

BETTER TO SEND HIM OFF TO A CO-ED CAMP FOR THE SUMMER WHEN HE'S 10 THAN TO WAIT UNTIL HE'S, SAY, 13 OR 14.

JASON WITH HORMONES. NOW THERE'S A SCARY THOUGHT.

I CAUGHT HIM DROOLING OVER PAIGE'S "COSMO" THE OTHER DAY, BUT APPARENTLY HE WAS JUST LOOKING AT A PENTIUM AD.

PETER! PETER! MOM AND DAD ARE LETTING ME GO TO SCIENCE CAMP THIS SUMMER!

COOL.

I MEAN, DID YOU CHECK OUT THIS BROCHURE?! IS THIS PLACE NOT PARADISE?!

WATERFALLS... HIKING TRAILS... CANOEING... A 3,000-YEAR-OLD REDWOOD GROVE... THIS DOES SOUND GREAT.

TREES, SCHMEES. GET TO THE PART ABOUT A T-1 LINE IN EVERY CABIN.

"THINGS TO PACK: FLASHLIGHT, INSECT REPELLANT, MATHEMATICA 3.0."

HERE'S A LIST OF WAYS TO ENTERTAIN QUINCY WHILE I'M GONE.

HERE'S A LIST OF TV SHOWS I'D LIKE YOU TO TAPE WHILE I'M GONE.

AND HERE'S A LIST OF CANDIES AND COOKIES I LIKE, JUST IN CASE YOU WERE THINKING OF SENDING ME CARE PACKAGES.

JASON, BY THE TIME I FINISH READING THESE, YOU'LL BE **HOME** FROM CAMP.

HMM. I SUPPOSE I COULD EDIT THOSE FIRST TWO LISTS DOWN SOME.

HOW NICE OF YOU TO INCLUDE THESE AIR-FREIGHT PHONE NUMBERS.

53

Panel 1: ARE YOU SURE THIS IS WHERE THE GIRLS' MAP SAYS TO MEET THEM? / YUP. THIS IS DEFINITELY THE SPOT.

Panel 2: BUT YOU CAN'T EVEN SEE HALF THE SKY OVER THOSE TREES! WHY WOULD THEY WANT US TO MEET THEM FOR STARGAZING **HERE**?!

Panel 3: ...UNLESS THEY NEVER **INTENDED** TO—... / **AAAA!** WE'RE STANDING IN A SEA OF POISON IVY!

Panel 4: THAT GIGGLING OFF IN THE BUSHES HAD BETTER JUST BE THE WIND!

Panel 5: I CAN'T BELIEVE EILEEN AND PHOEBE WOULD **PULL** SUCH A WRETCHED STUNT!

Panel 6: MAKING A FAKE MAP SO WE'D WANDER SMACK INTO THREE ACRES OF SOLID POISON IVY... WHAT THEY DID WAS THE PRODUCT OF SICK, TWISTED MINDS!

Panel 7: IT WAS ROTTEN AND SINISTER AND CRUEL AND DEPRAVED AND CALLOUS AND WICKED AND DOWNRIGHT MEAN!

Panel 8: COULD IT BE, MARCUS, THAT SOME GIRLS AREN'T SO BAD AFTER ALL? / SPEAK FOR YOURSELF. I HAD A LEAF UP MY SHORTS.

Panel 9: SO, BOYS, SEEN ANY GOOD CONSTELLATIONS LATELY? / MAYBE GULLIBLUS MAJOR? OR BRAINIUS MINOR?

Panel 10: WE SPENT HALF THE NIGHT SCRUBBING THAT POISON IVY OFF OUR SKIN! IT WASN'T AT ALL FUNNY! YOU GUYS ARE **SICK!** / MARK MY WORDS, GIRLS, THAT BEFORE THIS CAMP IS OVER, MARCUS AND I SHALL WREAK OUR VENGEANCE! YOU HAVE MESSED WITH THE WRONG TWO HONCHOS!

Panel 11: OOO... HOW TERRIFYING. / LOOK, PHOEBE— I'M SHAKING. / IF IT'S ANY CONSOLATION, YOU WOULD'VE SCARED ME. / **HEY, I'M SERIOUS!**

Panel 1: NOW THEY'VE DONE IT! NOW THEY'VE GONE TOO FAR! PBBSPT! PBBSPT!

Panel 2: FIRST THEY TRICKED US INTO THAT FIELD OF POISON IVY! THEN THEY GOT US TO DIVE INTO THE SWAMP! BUT PUTTING PEPPER IN OUR PUDDING CUPS AT DINNER JUST PLAIN CROSSES THE LINE! AND THE WAY THEY SAT THERE LAUGHING!

DINING HALL

Panel 3: I MEAN, WHO DO EILEEN AND PHOEBE THINK THEY **ARE**?!?

Panel 4: ...US?? I'D SAY THEY'RE OUR EQUALS, EXCEPT WE'RE GETTING WHOOPED.

AMEND

Panel 5: WHAT'S THAT? THE RULES FOR THE BIG CAMP BOHRMORE SCIENCE CONTEST.

PHYSICS

Panel 6: "WORKING IN TEAMS OF TWO, APPLY ONE OR MORE OF THE SCIENTIFIC PRINCIPLES YOU'VE LEARNED THIS SUMMER IN THE DESIGN AND EXECUTION OF AN EXPERIMENT OR DEMONSTRATION OF YOUR CHOOSING." COOL... THERE'S EVEN A BIG TROPHY!

AMEND

Panel 7: MARCUS, YOU AND I ARE GOING TO WIN THIS PRIZE. ASSUMING WE CAN SOMEHOW BEAT THAT STUPID EUGENE.

Panel 8: STUPID? *MOI*? DO I NEED TO SHOW YOU MY TRANSCRIPT AGAIN? HEY, EUGENE— I HEAR THERE ARE SOME AMAZING PROTOZOANS AT THE BOTTOM OF THE LAKE. HERE. YOU CAN BORROW MY MICROSCOPE.

Panel 9: HOW'S YOUR BIG SCIENCE PROJECT COMING ALONG? FINE. GO AWAY, EUGENE.

Panel 10: "FINE"? THAT'S TOO BAD, BECAUSE THE PROJECT HAWKINS AND I ARE DOING IS COMING ALONG **GLORIOUSLY**. IT'S GOING TO TAKE MUCH MORE THAN "FINE" TO BEAT ME IN THIS CONTEST.

Panel 11: EUGENE, YOU NIMROD! YOU LEFT THE CAP OFF THIS TEST TUBE OVERNIGHT, AND NOW OUR MOLARITY'S ALL MESSED UP!

AMEND

Panel 12: STILL, WE'RE DOING BETTER THAN "FINE." MARCUS, PASS ME THOSE ELECTRODES. TRUST ME— GO AWAY, EUGENE.

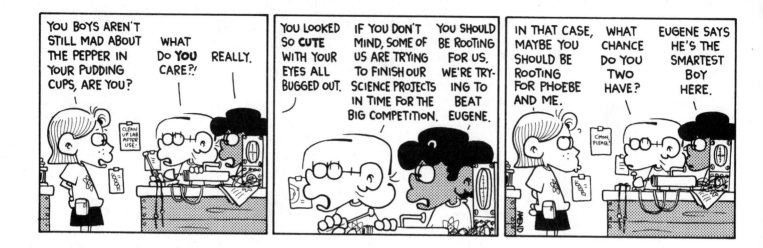

FoxTrot
BILL AMEND

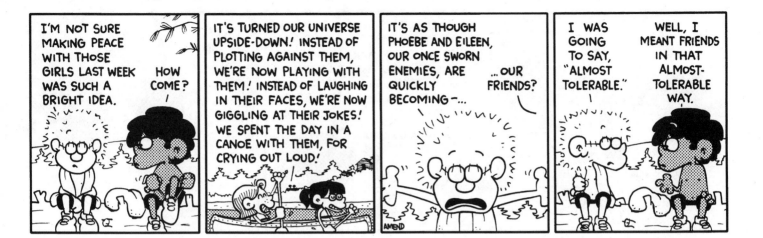

66

FoxTrot
BILL AMEND

69

WELL, IT'S BEEN A COUPLE OF MONTHS SINCE I'VE DONE THIS. LET'S SEE IF I'VE STILL GOT IT.

RIP! SLASH! AIEEE! WHAP! WHAP! SPLAT!

YOU HAVE BEEN TRANSFORMED INTO A POOL OF HUMAN BLOOD. GAME OVER.

DANG. I GUESS PLAYING "DOOMATHON" IS NOT LIKE RIDING A BIKE.

UNLESS YOU COUNT THE TIME PETER WENT DOWN HILL STREET WITH NO HANDS.

SO, HOW WAS THE FOOD AT CAMP?

INDESCRIBABLE.

IT SEEMED LIKE EVERY OTHER MEAL, YOU'D HAVE NO IDEA WHAT STRANGE CONCOCTION YOU WERE EATING.

NOT AT ALL LIKE MOM'S COOKING.

WOULD YOU BOYS PREFER YOUR EGGPLANT WAFFLES DRY OR WITH GRAVY?

...WHERE YOU KNOW ALL TOO WELL.

AT LEAST WITH MYSTERY MEAT, THERE'S A CHANCE YOU'LL LUCK OUT.

SO, WITH PETER WORKING AT A MOVIE THEATER, HAVE YOU BEEN ABLE TO SEE FILMS FOR FREE ALL SUMMER?

NO. NICOLE AND I TRIED TO SNEAK IN EARLY ON, BUT IT TURNED OUT TO BE A BIG WASTE OF TIME.

SEEMS OUR BROTHER IS SOMETHING OF THE LOW MAN ON THE TOTEM POLE.

TELL YOU WHAT— IF YOU WAIT UNTIL MY BOSS TAKES HIS BREAK, I CAN GET YOU IN TO SEE THE RESTROOMS.

PAIGE, YOU PROMISED ME "AIR FORCE ONE"!

PETER, PLEASE? HOW 'BOUT IF WE DROP THE PART ABOUT FREE JUMBO NACHOS?

SERVICE ENTRANCE

FoxTrot
BILL AMEND

Panel 1: JASON, IF YOU WANT TO BLOW THE $20 MOM GAVE YOU ON COMIC BOOKS AND CANDY, THAT'S YOUR BUSINESS. ALL I KNOW IS THAT *I'M* BUYING SCHOOL SUPPLIES.

PETER! NO! PLEASE!

Panel 2: IF YOU COME HOME WITH NOTEBOOKS AND PENCILS AND ALL I HAVE ARE COMICS AND THIS, I'M GOING TO LOOK INCREDIBLY IRRESPONSIBLE! PLEASE DON'T ONLY BUY SCHOOL SUPPLIES! PLEASE? PLEASE? PLEASE?

Panel 3: JASON, I GAVE MOM MY WORD. SORRY.

AND PEOPLE SAY *YOUNGER* BROTHERS ARE ANNOYING.

Panel 4: AND YOU THINK THEY'RE *WRONG*??

HOW CAN YOU SAY NO TO THE SMELL OF BLUE WATERMELON GUM?? DO YOU HAVE A COLD?

Panel 5: YOU'RE REALLY BUYING SCHOOL SUPPLIES?

YUP.

Panel 6: AARGH! I CAN'T BELIEVE YOU'RE DOING THIS TO ME! THE BUYING SPREE OF A LIFETIME, THWARTED BY MY BOY SCOUT OF A BROTHER!

Panel 7: THE CHANCE TO BUY COMIC BOOKS... GUM BY THE BOX... THE NEW G.I. JIM NINJA STAR SET... ALL SQUANDERED BECAUSE *YOU* HAD TO PROMISE MOM WE WOULDN'T MISSPEND HER MONEY!

Panel 8: WAIT A MINUTE! YOUR SHOELACES WERE CROSSED! WE'VE GOT OURSELVES A LOOPHOLE!

GIVE IT UP, F. LEE. THE NOTEBOOKS ARE THATAWAY.

All Tamagouchies 90% off

Panel 9: HOW WAS SHOPPING FOR SCHOOL SUPPLIES?

WELL, JASON WAS IN TYPICAL FORM.

Panel 10: I IMAGINE HE WANTED TO SPEND THE ENTIRE $20 I GAVE HIM ON COMIC BOOKS AND THE LIKE.

GEE, HOW'D YOU GUESS?

Panel 11: I TAKE IT HE EVENTUALLY CAME AROUND.

ONCE HE SAW THE AISLES OF "PLASMA MAN" NOTEBOOKS AND PENCILS.

Panel 12: IT KILLS ME TO SAY THIS, BUT THANK GOD FOR LICENSING.

PERSONALLY, I WENT WITH THE "BABE-WATCH" LINE OF PRODUCTS.

I FOUND A COUPLE DOLLARS IN MY DRESSER. CAN WE GO BACK FOR MORE?

78

MOM! MOM! GUESS WHAT?!

WHAT?

MISS O'MALLEY SAID MARCUS AND I COULD BE THE A-V BOYS FOR OUR CLASS THIS FALL!

A-V BOYS?

AUDIO-VISUAL. WE'LL BE IN CHARGE OF SETTING UP THE EQUIPMENT FOR SHOWING FILMS AND STUFF IN CLASS. IT'LL BE A LOT OF WORK, BUT I THINK IT'LL BE FUN.

WELL, I'M SURE YOU'RE UP TO THE TASK.

WE'RE RUNNING THE SURROUND SOUND CABLES TOMORROW.

REMIND ME TO START SCREENING MY PHONE CALLS AGAIN.

I'M THINKING WE'RE GOING TO NEED FIVE OR SIX BIG SPEAKERS.

MARCUS, MARCUS, MARCUS.

MAYBE THAT'S FINE FOR **TRADITIONAL** SURROUND SOUND SETUPS, BUT I THOUGHT WE WERE TRYING TO RAISE THE BAR HERE. JMX·SOUND™ SHOULD BE SOMETHING TOTALLY NEW.

WHEN WE FIRST TURN ON THAT MOVIE PROJECTOR, I WANT OUR CLASSMATES TO **KNOW** IT.

I MEANT FIVE OR SIX SPEAKERS PER STUDENT.

OK, NOW WE'RE ON THE SAME PAGE.

MISS O'MALLEY SAYS THIS IS THE PROJECTOR YOU AND I WILL BE IN CHARGE OF RUNNING.

SHE SAID IT WAS PRETTY SIMPLE TO OPERATE.

JUST YOUR BASIC 16mm.

YUP, YUP.

NO FANCY LENSES... NO FANCY ELECTRONICS... NO FANCY AUDIO OUTPUT JACKS... NO GIZMOS THAT A NOVICE MIGHT FIND FRIGHTENINGLY COMPLEX.

NOT YET, ANYWAY.

SO, DO YOU WANT TO DRILL THROUGH THE BACK OR THE FRONT?

TOOLS

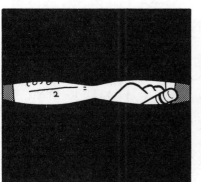

Panel 4: I KEEP FORGETTING TO TAKE MY GUM OUT BEFORE DINNER.

Panel 5:
PETER, WHAT DO YOU WANT FOR LUNCH TODAY?

OH, GOSH, I DUNNO...

Panel 6:
PEANUT BUTTER AND JELLY WOULD BE GOOD... BOLOGNA AND CHEESE WOULD BE GOOD... TURKEY... TUNA... HAM... SALAMI... THAT EGG SALAD YOU SOMETIMES MAKE...

Panel 7:
SO, ANY OF THOSE?

NO, NO— ALL OF THOSE.

Panel 8:
DID I MENTION I SAW OUR GROCER TEST-DRIVING A PORSCHE LAST WEEK?

YOU KNOW, THESE "FAMILY-SIZED" BOXES ARE GROSSLY MISLABELED.

Panel 9:
JASON, YOUR STUPID IGUANA GOT OUT OF HIS STUPID CAGE AGAIN!

Panel 10:
HE SLIPPED INTO MY ROOM, INTO MY CLOSET, AND CHEWED UP THE BRAND-NEW PINK CARDIGAN THAT WAS **GOING** TO GET ME A BOYFRIEND THIS YEAR!

Panel 11:
I WANT TO KNOW WHAT YOU'RE GOING TO DO ABOUT THIS!

PROBABLY GIGGLE ALL NIGHT LONG.

Panel 12:
WHOEVER THE IDIOT WAS WHO SAID "HONESTY IS THE BEST POLICY"...

I DON'T NEED THE SWEATER BACK, BY THE WAY.

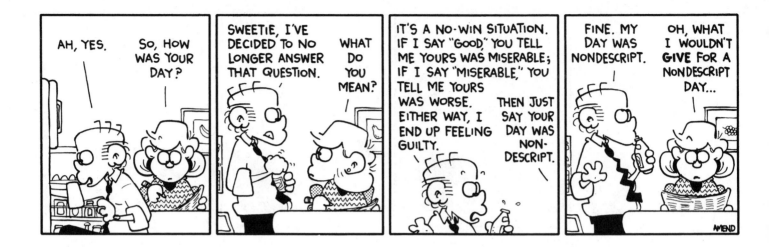

94

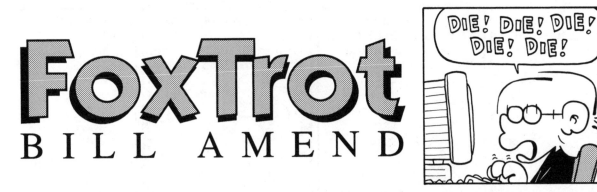

WHAT DO YOU **MEAN** YOU WON'T LET ME WATCH YOU PLAY?!

THE INSTRUCTIONS SAY NOT TO SHOW THE RIVIABLO BETA TO ANYONE.

PAIGE, I DON'T THINK YOU UNDERSTAND! I'VE BEEN WAITING FOUR YEARS FOR THIS GAME TO COME OUT!

THE KNOWLEDGE THAT IT'S RUNNING ON OUR COMPUTER AND I CAN'T SEE IT WILL **KILL** ME! I'LL BURST AT THE SEAMS! I'LL KNOW PAIN LIKE NO HUMAN COULD POSSIBLY ENDURE!

...OR MAYBE THE PROBLEM IS THAT YOU **DO** UNDERSTAND.

WELL PUT.

CLICK

OOO—THIS GAME IS AMAZING!

OOO—THIS GAME IS INCREDIBLE!

OOO—THIS GAME IS SOOOO GOOOOD!

AT LEAST THE PACKAGING IS. READY TO OPEN IT?

OOO—THIS GAME IS UNNBELIEEEVABLE!

PAIGE, THE ENVELOPE I'M SLIPPING UNDER THE DOOR CONTAINS MY LIFE'S SAVINGS...

WHAT'S THAT?

IT'S A LETTER FROM THE PRESIDENT OF BLIZZERBUND SOFTWARE.

NO WAY! WHAT'S IT SAY? WHAT'S IT SAY?

"DEAR MS. FOX, THANK YOU FOR YOUR EVALUATION OF OUR RIVIABLO CD-ROM BETA."

"PER YOUR SUGGESTIONS, THE FINAL VERSION OF THE GAME WILL HAVE LESS VIOLENCE, CUTER MONSTERS, AND SIGNIFICANTLY EASIER PUZZLES.

"P.S. THANKS ESPECIALLY FOR THE GREAT IDEA TO CHANGE THE GAME'S TITLE TO 'HAPPY TOWN.'"

I THOUGHT THEY SENT YOU A FORM LETTER.

OOPS. YOU'RE RIGHT. I MUST'VE MISREAD IT.

JASON, WILL YOU STOP BAWLING LONG ENOUGH TO TELL ME WHAT'S WRONG?!

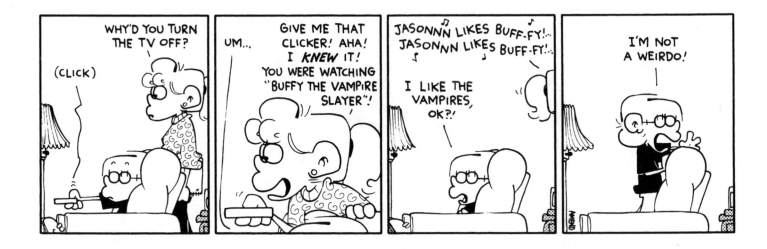

117

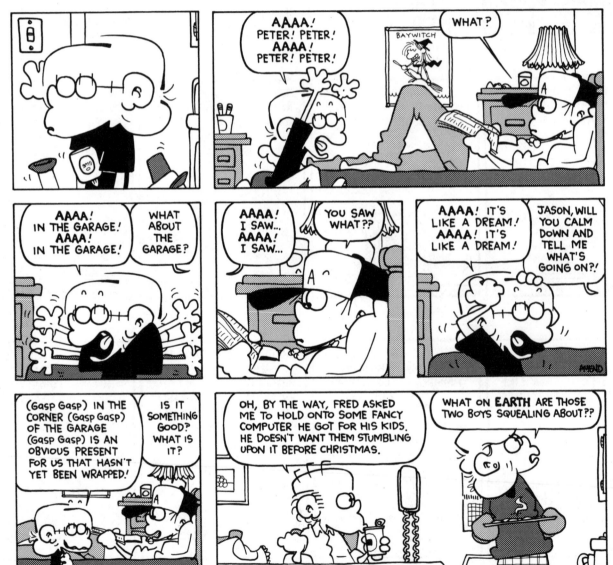